Armies of the Vietnam War (2)

Lee E Russell • Illustrated by Mike Chappell

Series editor Martin Windrow

First published in Great Britain in 1983 by
Osprey Publishing, Elms Court, Chapel Way, Botley,
Oxford OX2 9LP, United Kingdom.
Email: info@ospreypublishing.com

Series Editor: MARTIN WINDROW

British Library Cataloguing in Publication Data

Armies of the Vietnam war.
  2
  1. Armies—Vietnam—History—20th century
  2. Vietnamese Conflict, 1961–1975—Campaigns
  I. Lee E. Russell
  355′.009597   DS556.2

CIP Data for this publication is available from
the British Library

ISBN 0-85045-514-6

Filmset in Great Britain
Printed in China through World Print Ltd.

FOR A CATALOGUE OF ALL BOOKS PUBLISHED BY
OSPREY MILITARY AND AVIATION PLEASE CONTACT:

The Marketing Manager, Osprey Direct UK,
PO Box 140, Wellingborough, Northants,
NN8 2FA, UnitedKingdom.
Email: info@ospreydirect.co.uk

The Marketing Manager, Osprey Direct USA,
c/o MBI Publishing, PO Box 1,
729 Prospect Avenue, Osceola, WI 54020, USA.
Email: info@ospreydirectusa.com

www.ospreypublishing.com

Acknowledgements

The author wishes to express his gratitude to Mr. M.
Albert Mendez and Mr. Tom Hunt, who gave un-
selfishly of their time and information, allowed me access
to their private collections and permitted me to repro-
duce items from their book. I would also like to thank
Mr. Adam Dintenfass, Mr. Severino Mendez, Jr., Mr.
Tom Bartlett of *Leatherneck Magazine*, and the personnel
of the US Army, Navy and Marine Corps Public Affairs
Offices in New York City for their assistance. Finally, a
special thanks to my fellow Vietnam veterans, former
Marines Chris DeSalvo, John Olsen and Michael Pahios,
and Mr. Jason Pilalas, former US Navy, for their help.
All opinions and conclusions, however, are the author's
own.

Introduction

The Vietnam War is a complex subject, even in so limited an aspect as military uniform. Nine armies fought there between 1962 and 1973, each with its own peculiarities. In this work it is only possible to examine in detail the uniforms and equipment of the major contenders, the United States, the Republic of Vietnam, and the Communist Democratic Republic of (North) Vietnam. The Viet Cong, military arm of the National Liberation Front and instigator of the original insurgency, is covered only incidentally. Of the five other Free World nations that provided troops, only the Republic of Korea is even mentioned. Regrettably, this choice had to be made for reasons of space. I have also chosen to concentrate on the various Allied élite forces at the expense of their more prosaic brethren. Readers should not assume that everyone in South-East Asia wore a camouflage suit!

I have also taken some liberties with official nomenclature, especially American terms. Contrary to popular belief, the US military does not designate every item with an M-prefixed number. Several systems are used, and in some cases I have also used the unofficial terminology of the troops themselves. Finally, when no convenient designation exists, I have made use of terms used by military collectors.

Readers who desire more information are referred to the select bibliography at the end, which includes works on the conflict itself as well as its uniforms. Material on other Allied armies, and on other units of the US forces, will be found in MAA 104, *Armies of the Vietnam War 1962–75*.

With face camouflaged, and wearing a 'tiger-stripe' uniform and 'Jones hat', a reconnaissance soldier wades a stream; even his M-16 is 'tiger-striped', apparently with paint. He is a member of the Aerorifle Platoon (ARP), 2/17 Cavalry, 101st Airborne Division: ARPs undertook short-range reconnaissance, evaluated air strikes, and provided security for downed aircraft. He is festooned with cotton bandoliers and grenades. A Pilot's Survival Knife is taped to his harness, and above it an empty film can, probably to hold matches. The knife is a poor choice of weapon, due to its short blade and sawtooth back. A field dressing pocket has been sewn to the left sleeve of the jacket; and note the yellow chamois leather work glove, a fairly common item. The rucksack is the ARVN two-pocket model. (US Army)

US Army Uniforms and Insignia

During the Vietnam period, the standard Army field uniform worldwide was the OG 107 Cotton Sateen Shirt and Trousers: OG 107 stood for Olive Green 107, the colour specification for the material. These were referred to interchangeably as 'fatigues' or 'utilities' by the troops. The trousers had four patch pockets, two side and two at the rear with buttoned flaps. The shirt had two breast pockets, closed with buttoned, rectangular flaps.

In the early 1960s, Secretary of Defense Robert S. McNamara instituted his 'commonability' programme to reduce the number of similar items in use by different services. It was decided that henceforth everyone would use the same fatigue clothing. A slightly modified version of the OG 107 utilities was selected. The trousers were the same, but the shirt's pocket flaps were now pointed and shirt-type buttoned cuffs replaced the earlier plain ones. This version was used by the Army, Air Force and Marines, and by certain shore-based units of the Navy (such as the Seabees—the Navy Construction Battalions). The Army supply system did not distinguish between this type and the earlier shirt.

The OG 107 fatigues were worn by the Army during the 'advisor period' and the initial deployment of combat troops to Vietnam. After the first year or so Army troops were ordered to take only one set with them to Vietnam and these were rarely worn in-country. What replaced them was the Jungle Utility Uniform (actually 'Coat and Trousers, Man's, Combat, Tropical'—although no one ever called it that). It had been designed personally by Lt.Gen. William P. Yarborough, commander of the Army's Special Warfare Center (later JFKCENMA) at Ft. Bragg, NC, in the early 1960s. Yarborough was well qualified for the task; as a young lieutenant in 1941, he had designed the Army's World War II paratroop uniform. Basically what he did 20 years later was to update his World War II design.

The original jungle utilities, made in 100% cotton poplin, began to be issued in Vietnam in the late summer of 1965. The jacket had four large bellows pockets, the top two slanted inwards for easy access under web gear; all closed with slanted flaps and exposed buttons. There was a waist adjustment tab at each side, a gas flap that counter-buttoned beneath the front fly, and shoulder straps. The sleeves had shirt-type cuffs. The trousers had seven pockets: two side, two rear, and two bellows-type cargo pockets on the legs. A seventh was located within the left cargo pocket. The leg and rear pockets closed with exposed-button flaps.

An early complaint concerned the snagging of web gear on the exposed buttons. The first modification to the uniform was to make all the buttons concealed. Shoulder straps, take-up tabs and gas flap were retained.

A final version of this uniform appeared in late 1967. The fabric was changed to 100% rip-stop cotton poplin, which had nylon filaments woven into the material at intervals. This model also standardised a simplified version of the jacket, with concealed buttons and shirt-type cuffs, but lacking gas flap, adjustment tabs or shoulder straps. Trousers remained unchanged from the concealed-button 'intermediate' pattern.

Since the late 1950s the Army had been wearing black leather combat boots. (Airborne troops had the slightly higher Corcoran paratroop boots instead.) Advisor experience in Vietnam suggested that something lighter was desirable. Several types were tested before the Hot Weather Tropical Boot—universally referred to as the 'Vietnam jungle boot'—was adopted. This was made of black leather and OD nylon duck, with a punji-spike-resistant aluminium insole. The original model issued in 1965 lacked a later ankle reinforcement. Very late in the war, a 'Panama tread' replaced the original sole.

During the 1965 deployment a temporary shortage of jungle boots was made up by an issue of M1945 Jungle Boots, in russet leather and canvas, with a buckled cuff top. In poor condition after years of storage, they quickly became unserviceable and vanished. The original leather combat boots were standard wear in-country during 1965–66, and saw occasional wear thereafter by individuals.

During the advisor period the standard Army fatigue cap was the private purchase 'Walker cap' with stiffened crown. In 1964 the Army replaced this with a silly-looking 'baseball' style model, the

OG 106 Hot Weather Cap. It was never popular with Army troops, who usually crushed the crown to make it more presentable. The Vietnamese were soon making a better-looking model, and this was immediately acquired by everyone from Gen. Westmoreland on down.

In 1967, the Tropical Hat was introduced, with all-around brim and loops for camouflage. Soon to be dubbed the 'boonie hat' after the 'boondocks' where the infantry operated, it was a popular and successful design. An accompanying insect net was immediately discarded. The hat could be worn in a variety of ways, many reminiscent of the Old West.

Throughout the Vietnam period the Army issued a black web waist belt with a solid rectangular buckle. A white T-shirt worn in the 'States was usually dyed green in Vietnam; in 1966 the Army began issuing OD models to troops going overseas.

Insignia

Insignia on combat clothing underwent several changes during the Vietnam War, including colour, presentation and, in some cases, design.

After 1957 Army fatigues were worn with a cloth

Early US operations were carried out in the OG 107 utility uniform worn here by men of the 173rd Airborne Brigade's 16th Armor in Binh Duong Province, September 1965. Note full-colour brigade patch and Sp4 insignia worn by radioman. The AN/PRC-25 was the standard radio throughout the war, and came with its own packframe, as here, although most RTOs soon learned to stuff it in a standard rucksack to deny the enemy such a conspicuous target—radiomen were often picked off as a priority. The soldier in the background can just be seen to wear the early exposed-button jungle utilities. (US Army)

nametape over each shirt pocket. The left read U.S. ARMY in yellow letters on a black background. The right was the individual's last name in black on a white background. In late 1966 the latter was changed to black on Olive Drab, and in mid-1967 the U.S. ARMY nametape followed suit. These changes affected only new issue at first, and it took about a year to change over completely.

There were also changes in rank insignia for both officers and enlisted men. In late 1966 the colours used in officers' rank insignia were changed from the embroidered white and yellow used on fatigue clothing to black and tan-khaki respectively. All officers' branch insignia was changed from yellow to black.

Enlisted men originally wore rank insignia as full-size items on shirt sleeves. The original colours were Army green and yellow; in 1967 this changed to

Soldiers of the 1st Bde., 101st Airborne Div. display a mixture of uniforms typical of the period—Operation 'Checkerboard', December 1965—and M-56 equipment. The central man wears OG 107 fatigues with full insignia and nametapes, and M1945 jungle boots; and note M1910 hatchet fixed to M1956 Entrenching Tool Carrier. The others seem to wear early exposed-button jungle fatigue jackets, and a mixture of jungle and standard fatigue trousers is worn—although officially prohibited. The two outside men wear either combat or paratroop boots in black leather; the left hand man has the early—and unreliable—LAW disposable rocket launcher slung. (US Army)

Olive Drab and black. Starting in 1967, some enlisted personnel in Vietnam began wearing locally authorised metal pin-on collar insignia. This became common by 1969 and regulation in 1971.

All of these changes were referred to as 'subdued' versions of the originals. Subdued unit insignia also appeared.

Camouflage Uniforms

The US Army originally saw no need for camouflage clothing, although it procured several patterns for the Vietnamese, which were occasionally worn by Army advisors. These were either commercial items intended for sportsmen, or products of the Army's own Equipment Research and Development Laboratories (ERDL).

After the arrival of US ground troops it became

'Tunnel Rats' of the 56th Engineer Demolition Team, 25th Inf.Div. display captured enemy equipment during Operation 'Wahiawa', May 1966. They wear M-56 equipment over M1952 Armor Vests and OD T-shirts. These early model vests were later modified, losing their shoulder straps and receiving an uncomfortable three-quarter collar. The central man has a white plastic C-ration spoon tucked in his equipment. A mixture of M-14 and M-16 rifles is evident; the captured weapon is the ChiCom Type 53 carbine. (US Army)

obvious that reconnaissance was going to be very important, and that some type of camouflage clothing was needed for this. As an interim measure, members of American élite units obtained locally-made camouflage uniforms from the small Vietnamese tailor shops that dotted the country. These could make you anything you wanted, but most customers elected either ARVN patterns or copies of US uniforms in camouflage material. Most were of 'tiger-stripe' patterns.

Eventually, in 1967, the Army introduced its

own design: the Coat and Trousers, Man's, Camouflage, Cotton. It was made in a green foliage ('leaf') pattern in rip-stop material. Styling was identical to that of the 'late' model tropical utilities and the OD 'boonie hat'. Intended for élite troops—Long Range Reconnaissance Patrols (LRRPs), Special Forces, ARPs, Pathfinders, Dog Handlers, etc.—it was initially in short supply. Even later, some personnel thought it less effective than the 'tiger-stripes' and continued to wear these. In addition to

Vietnamese patterns, 'tiger-stripe' items from other Asian countries such as Thailand and Japan were also worn at times.

US Army Equipment

All American military personnel were issued the M-1 Steel Helmet. This came in two parts, an outer 'steel pot' and an inner fibre liner. With it was issued a reversible camouflage cover and an elastic retaining band. (Intended to hold foliage, it was usually used to carry small personal items in the field.) The camouflage covers were usually decorated with graffiti, with calendars, home town names and personal mottoes or nicknames the most popular.

Reconnaissance troops of 1/9 Cav., 1st Cav.Div. (Airmobile), November 1970. Arrangement of equipment is typical, as is use of bootlaces to secure trouser legs tightly below the knee. Note use of bulky but capacious canteen carriers as ammo pouches. M-16s are camouflaged both with paint (left hand man) and taped cloth (rifle with 30-round magazine leaning against CONEX, far left). (US Army)

The standard Army web gear was the M1956 pattern. It consisted of Pistol Belt, 'H'-type Belt Suspenders, Field Pack, OD Plastic Canteen with Carrier, Field Dressing Pouch, Entrenching Tool Carrier and Universal Small Arms Ammunition Pouches. The latter held either two M-14 rifle magazines, or four M-16 magazines, or five 30-round magazines for the M-1 carbine, or 25 12-gauge shotgun shells. Two grenades could be carried externally, and two more within, if the pouch was used for this purpose.

The M1956 equipment stood up well to Vietnam, the Field Pack alone proving too small for practical use. Its replacement was the Lightweight Tropical Rucksack. In 1969 a tropical version of the

III MAF commander Lt.Gen. Herman Nickerson Jr. inspects a Recon unit of 1st Marine Div. in 1969. His locally-made utility cap in leaf-pattern camouflage has metal pin-on rank insignia; the USMC adopted a somewhat similar cap as standard in the late 1970s. Note ARVN I Corps patch, a red 'I' on white, tagged to right breast pocket; the commander of III MAF was automatically Senior Advisor to the ARVN forces in MR I. The plastic bottle hung from the holster contains earplugs, usually worn only by artillerymen. The Recon Marine wears leaf-pattern utilities and 'boonie hat', with the Marine version of the STABO harness, and M-56 equipment. (USMC)

Men of Co.B, 3rd Recon Bn., 3rd Marine Div. patrol below the Western DMZ on New Year's Day, 1969. The leading Marine wears 'duck hunter' camouflage fatigues and a black beret. He carries both M26A1 and M-59 fragmentation grenades on his M-56 equipment; lacking a knife, he has taped an M-7 bayonet to his gear, and green tape camouflages his rifle. The second man has taped a cleaning rod to his rifle, for emergencies. (USMC)

M-56 equipment was introduced, but never in large quantity. Another wartime innovation was a special ammunition vest for M-79 grenadiers, which held 24 rounds. Two versions of the M1952 Armor Vest, made of ballistic nylon, were issued. (This was usually referred to as a 'flak vest' by troops.) All these items are illustrated and described in the photos and colour plates.

M-16 rifle ammunition was issued in the field in stripper clips packed in OD cotton bandoliers. Troops usually loaded the ammunition into spare magazines and carried these in the bandoliers. 40mm grenades also came in bandoliers, and these were used as they came. M-60 machine gun ammunition came in linked belts, either loose, packed in flimsy cardboard boxes inside OD cotton carriers, or in ammo cans. All of these were used,

Belt for personnel armed with the M-1 rifle—each pocket held one eight-round 'enbloc' clip; the six-pocket M1937 BAR Magazine Belt holding 12 20-round BAR magazines; and the M1936 Pistol Belt, for personnel carrying other weapons. With these came either M1936 or M1945 Belt Suspenders, both of 'X'-type configuration. The M1945 type differed from the earlier model in having padding and a provision for attaching the M1945 Combat Pack. It also lacked the 'D'-rings provided at the front of the M1936 type.

The M1945 Combat Pack had been developed by the Army in World War II and had many features copied from the contemporary Marine Corps Haversack. Among these were ties at top and sides to attach bedroll-type items, and provision to carry an entrenching tool in the M1943 Carrier on the pack flap. There was a small external pocket on the right side. It attached to the M1945 Belt Suspenders by a complicated system of straps and 'D'-rings. (The ARVN, being practical people, simply improvised permanent packstraps and wore the pack knapsack-fashion.)

Other items, such as bayonet scabbards and canteens, hung below the belts, attached by horizontal hooks (the M1910 Fastener) to grommets on the belts. Still other items, such as the M-1 Carbine Magazine Carrier, slipped on over the pistol belt by means of a loop on their backs.

Accompanied by his Vietnamese counterpart, a USMC captain sets about his advisory duties with the 2nd VNMC Bn. at Can Duoc, 35 miles south of Saigon, in late 1964. Both officers wear 'tiger-stripe' uniform with the single-button shirt pockets characteristic of the VNMC, and utility caps, and both carry .45 pistols in shoulder holsters. The US officer has pin-on captain's bars on both collar points, and a USMC frame buckle on a black Army web belt. The VNMC major wears his naval-style rank insignia attached to a shirt button, French fashion, and a smaller version is sewn to his cap. Nametapes are in battalion colour. (S. Stibbens, *Leatherneck* **Magazine**)

but since the weapon was belt-fed its ammunition was usually carried wrapped around the body, bandolier-style. When you needed the gun, there was no time to start unpacking its belt! M-14 ammunition was normally carried only in magazines, but was issued in stripper clips.

The US Army World War II/Korean War Field Gear

During the Vietnam period, these equipments were used by the ARVN, the Koreans and (in part) by the US Marines.

Items included the ten-pocket M1936 Cartridge

US Marine Corps Combat Uniforms and Insignia

In the early 1960s, in common with the rest of the armed forces, the Marine Corps had been required to adopt the Army's standard OG 107 utility uniform. (The Marines, incidentally, never use the term 'fatigues'.) These were to replace a Marine pattern in use since the early 1950s. The changeover was not yet complete by the time of Vietnam and both uniforms were still in service.

The earlier Marine utilities came in two versions,

one in heavy twill and another in HBT cloth (Herringbone Twill—a material used since World War II for American combat clothing). The shirt had plain cuffs and two breast pockets closed with pointed flaps. A map pocket was concealed beneath the left side. All buttons were concealed. The trousers, also in two versions, had normal side pockets and two plain patch rear ones. The left rear pocket only was closed by a button.

The OG 107 utilities that replaced this uniform have already been described.

Both uniforms received in Marine service a stencil on the left shirt pocket—the Marine Corps' globe and anchor insignia with the letters USMC below, all in black.

The Marine Corps in Vietnam did not distin-guish between types of utility uniforms, and they were worn in whatever combination the individual desired. The Corps additionally permitted shirt sleeves to be cut off at the elbows, something not condoned by the Army after about 1964. White cotton T-shirts were worn beneath.

The characteristic Marine utility cap, made in

ARVN Rangers board a US Army CH-21 helicopter in February 1963. They wear American OG 107 fatigues, and a mixture of headgear: steel helmets, maroon berets, a French bush hat and a 'baseball' fatigue cap. Equipment is limited to pistol belts and M1945 suspenders; the weapons are M-1 carbines and a .45 automatic, though somewhere out of frame there ought to be a BAR as well. The 20-round carbine magazines are carried in two-magazine pouches; one man has an obsolescent AN/PRC-6 'walkie-talkie'. The 2nd Lt. (*Thieu Uy*) in the bush hat has his metal Ranger Badge pinned above the right breast pocket. (US Army)

ARVN Rangers of either the 30th or the 38th Bn. carry a wounded prisoner to safety during the Saigon street fighting of Tet 1968. The left hand man wears OG 107 fatigues, and on his right shoulder the patch of the US 199th Light Inf. Bde., indicating past service with them in some capacity. The other two Rangers wear 'duck hunter' fatigues. Note Ranger star-and-panther insignia painted on helmets. (Former RVN: author's collection)

jackets were left plain. (Some individuals, however, apparently added the insignia on their own with a marker pen.) In the urgency and confusion of the first year, Marine commanders had no objection to the mixing of jungle and ordinary utility uniforms, and in fact paid little attention to such things during the whole war. 1965 was a hard year logistically, and some smaller Marines even ended up wearing ARVN utilities.

In 1968 the Marine Corps decided to adopt the new leaf-pattern camouflage utilities for all Marines in Vietnam, and issue began at the end of the year. Transition took over a year and, in the interim, the mixing of camouflage and standard jungle utilities was allowed.

Throughout the whole period the Marines retained their original utility cap, but OD and camouflage boonie hats were also worn. The white T-shirts gave way to olive and sometimes the tan-khaki web belts were dyed green as well. Jungle boots appeared in early 1966 and gradually supplanted the black leather ones in-country.

The élite Marine Force Recon units generally followed a similar evolution to that of other élite forces. Starting out with ordinary utilities, they gradually obtained locally-made 'tiger-stripe' and 'duck hunter' camouflage suits, and finally, leaf-pattern uniforms.

The author recalls that in summer 1968 black T-shirts were a common affectation among Marine Combined Action Platoons (CAPs)—squad-sized units that lived in Vietnamese villages to support the local militia.

Marine enlisted rank insignia were displayed as brass pin-on devices on the shirt collar. These were black when issued, but wore down to bare metal in use. Marine officers used metal pin-on insignia of exactly the same patterns as Army officers (but slightly smaller in size) and these were worn on the collar as well, on both points since Marine officers have no 'branch'. Naturally, insignia were usually removed in the field.

olive green twill with a stiffened front, came with the globe and anchor stencilled at the front. Footwear, since the early 1960s, was the standard black leather combat boot used by all the other services. One distinguishing feature of the Marine combat uniform was a tan-khaki web belt with a brass frame buckle (black when issued but usually worn to bare metal in service).

The OG 107 uniform was worn in Vietnam from 1965 on, although after the first year or so its use was confined to rear area personnel. The older utilities disappeared completely during the first year. Once in Vietnam the Marines received the same jungle utilities as everyone else, in all the variations that existed. Lacking the stencil for the pocket, the

ARVN Ranger captain and his radioman, c.1962. The officer wears fatigues and a 'baseball' cap in the so-called 'SAS pattern' camouflage. Note Ranger patches on both the left shoulder and the camouflage scarf. The ARVN parachutist's brevet is worn in both metal and cloth, on cap and right breast respectively, and metal ranking on cap and left breast. The .45 holster has added cartridge loops on the strap. The radioman wears OG 107 utilities, or a local copy, and a 'tiger-stripe' hat. (US Army)

Marine Corps Equipment

Marine personal equipment in Vietnam was a mixture of Army patterns and some unique designs of their own, many approaching obsolesence.

Last-minute briefing for ARVN Rangers from 52nd CAB Pathfinders, November 1970. Organic to larger Aviation units, Pathfinder Detachments were élite infantry responsible for selecting and marking helicopter LZs, and co-ordination of the landing operation. The Pathfinders here (second and fourth from left) wear leaf-pattern fatigues, one with a black T-shirt of which the significance is unknown; note also the unusual nametapes, with light lettering on a dark background. The US helicopter crewman (third from left) wears the two-piece Nomex flight suit, an M1951 Field Jacket, and aircrew 'chickenplate' armour vest. The Rangers wear mostly leaf-pattern fatigues, though one has OG 107s; M-56 equipment, and ARVN two-pocket rucksacks. The third from the right displays the rifle sling worn in 'assault' style, with one loop through the rear sling swivel and around the stock and a second around the front sight post, allowing the rifle to be carried ready for action. Helmets are camouflaged with paint, and the left hand man wears his maroon beret inside out for reduced visibility. Centre is a VNAF pilot or liaison officer: the ARVN had no aviation component, and all helicopter crews were VNAF personnel. He wears a light grey L-2B Flight Jacket over his camouflage fatigues. (US Army)

The M-1 Steel Helmet was issued with a mixture of camouflage covers. The reversible Army type was standard, but many Marines received the older World War II/Korea pattern, exclusive to the Corps. This used similar colours but in a different pattern. Initially, camouflage retaining bands were made up from old rubber inner tubes; later, the Army camouflage bands became available.

The Marine rifleman went to Vietnam equipped with the M-14. With this he received a Marine M1961 Rifle Belt and four M1961 Ammunition Pouches, each holding one 20-round magazine. The rifle belt had a series of snaps down the centre to secure the pouches. To the belt was attached the rest of the equipment: usually, two World War II/Korea aluminium canteens in M1910 carriers, the Marine Jungle First Aid Kit, and a bayonet in a scabbard (the last usually attached to the bottom of an ammunition pouch). The belt was supported by

suspenders, the most common of which was a World War II Marine pattern consisting of two separate straps crossing at the back in an 'X'; as the straps were separate, it was necessary to tie them together with wire or string where they crossed at the back. The M1943 Entrenching Tool and Carrier were standard.

In the early period two further items were common issue: M1942 Field Dressing Pouches and World War II Three-Pocket Grenade Carriers. The latter was of much greater use to the Marine than the soldier, since the former's web gear made no provision for the safe carrying of hand grenades.

The Marine pack system was a leftover from World War II and could be made up in four different configurations. In the field the only one used was the Light Marching Pack, which comprised just the Haversack. Unlike Army packs, it could be worn without the rest of the equipment on

knapsack-type straps. Again, unlike Army packs, it was simply a bag whose top folded over and was held in place by two buckled straps. Other items could be stored externally under the fold; usually this might include a nylon rain poncho or the World War II Marine Camouflage Shelter Half.

A common Marine item was a US Navy Rain Jacket with two slash patch pockets. The author was unable to discover if this was an issue item or something that was 'acquired' unofficially.

Instructors from Co.L, 75th Infantry, the LRRP unit of 101st Airborne Div., teach rappelling techniques to the *'Hac Bao'* ('Black Panthers') of the ARVN 1st Div. Strike Company. As members of a Ranger unit the Americans wear black berets; the central figure wears his with the silver Parachutist Badge above the 75th Inf. crest. Right hand man wears Airborne and Ranger tabs above the divisional patch. The ARVN troops wear Vietnamese leaf-pattern fatigues, with full-colour blue and white divisional patches on the left sleeve and company patches on the right breast pocket; and silver-badged black berets. (US Army)

The Marines issued two versions of their own M1955 Armor Vest. This used for protection a series of overlapping fibreglass plates, bonded by a thermosetting polyester resin. The front closure had both a zipper and snaps. A reinforced and eyeletted band around the bottom allowed the attachment of equipment with M1910-type fasteners. There was also a very useful 'rope ridge' on the right shoulder that prevented a slung rifle from slipping off while on the march. A separate lower piece, designed to protect the groin, was worn only by helicopter crews, if at all.

The early model vest had only one pocket, on the left breast. Later on, two additional pockets were crudely attached to the lower front of the vest, each closed with a pointed flap. Both types were used throughout the war. Some Marines elected to wear the rest of their equipment over the vest, allowing it all to be shucked off as one piece. Most, however, wore the vest on top.

Once in Vietnam, the Marines quickly 'acquired' the superior Army M1956 equipment. The 'doggie' suspenders in particular were much prized. Once the M-16 came into use the M1961 equipment was inadequate, and those Marines unable to obtain M1956 universal pouches made do with bandoliers. The Marine pack proved inadequate, and those Marines who tried the Army's equivalent M1956 found it little better. Fibre packboards of World War II vintage were used as an interim measure. By 1969 most Marines were using Army Lightweight Rucksacks, ARVN two-pocket models or even NVA rucksacks instead. Like the Army, the Marines discovered that empty Claymore mine bags made handy musettes. The Marines showed little interest in the Army flak vest, although some were used. All of these items, except for the Claymore bags, entered Marine inventory through

A student taking part in a National Police Field Force training class in August 1970 wears tightly-tailored 'leopard' camouflage fatigues, cotton magazine bandoliers and an ARVN three-pocket rucksack. His US helmet cover is worn 'brown side out', the colours and pattern coincidentally matching those of the uniform. (US Army)

very unofficial channels, the phrase 'beg, borrow or steal' being most descriptive; and the Marines always had VC/NVA souvenirs to trade.

ARVN Uniforms and Insignia

The standard ARVN field uniform was of similar design to the American OG 107 fatigues, although a close inspection would reveal differences in material, cut and stitching. Local tailoring produced slight variations (usually shoulder straps or additional pockets), and it was the practice of regular troops to have their uniforms tailored to a tight fit. Fatigue trousers were often worn outside the boots.

A class in extraction techniques conducted by men of the US Army's 283rd Helicopter Detachment in 1969. They wear two-piece Nomex flight suits and locally-made 'baseball' caps, with full-colour embroidered insignia to personal taste; the man second from left has full-colour Aviator's wings and unit title. The left hand man wears the unit patch on his pocket, and a locally-made ('beercan') metal crest version on his cap. The subdued patch of 44th Medical Bde. worn on the right shoulder indicates a previous combat tour with that unit. He wears the .38 revolver issued to aircrew, in a locally-made black leather holster. The ARVN troops wear leaf-pattern utilities, and the shoulder title worn by the right hand man identifies 2nd Ranger Group. ARVN officers in the background can just be seen to wear ranking in different positions, either on the shirt front or the collar points. (US Army)

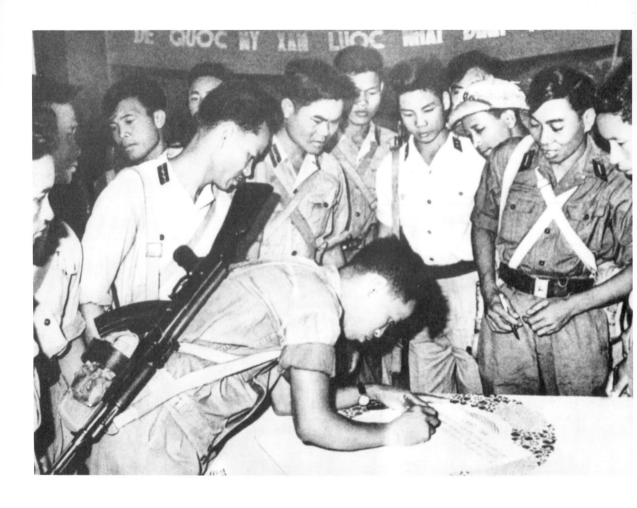

NVA soldiers sign a petition of support, in about 1965. Most have khaki uniforms, but some wear the white dress shirt seen only in the North. The man with the slung AK-47 wears the rare NVA shirt with a battledress-style waistband, sometimes called the 'NVA Combat Jacket' by Americans. Sam Browne belts without cross straps identify the two right hand men as officers; and note use of collar tabs by the officers, NCOs and enlisted men in this photo—see chart on a later page. (Tom Hunt Collection)

Starting in the early 1960s, with the deepening of the National Emergency, the fatigue uniform was also worn as service dress. Originally issued just to the Army, this uniform was eventually used by virtually every branch of military and paramilitary forces.

In the late 1960s American-made jungle utilities began to be issued to the Vietnamese. They were generally of the later patterns, and never entirely superseded the earlier uniform.

Standard headgear was either the Vietnamese fatigue cap or an American boonie hat. Units authorised berets wore them French-style, pulled to the left. US combat or jungle boots were provided by the Americans.

Élite and paramilitary forces, especially in the Mekong Delta, made extensive use of camouflage clothing. In addition to American patterns many indigenous types existed. In theory, some organisations (the Airborne and Marines, for example) had their own patterns. However, for most ARVN units the source of such uniforms was a local tailor shop. Troops often selected whatever appealed to them, or simply what was available. Lower level troops might wear patterns discarded by a different organisation. (For example, the author has a photograph of a Popular Forces soldier in 1969 wearing a worn-out French 'lizard' camouflage jacket as formerly used by the Presidential Bodyguard, who had adopted another pattern.) Two weights of cloth existed, a lightweight cotton and a heavy twill. Styling varied widely, but the most common type resembled the standard fatigue uniform in cut, with added trouser pockets. There were also a variety of different pocket details to be

seen. It should be remembered that strict enforcement of dress regulations was never a high priority in the ARVN.

The Vietnamese Army had an enormous variety of shoulder patches. Each corps, division, school and command had its own, but so did every regiment, battalion and élite company (either independent or divisional) within the Army. Other patches commemorated participation in certain difficult campaigns, such as the 1972 defence of An Loc. Designs could be simple or quite complex. Most were made in full colour; subdued versions appeared in the early 1970s. In a work of this size it would be ludicrous to attempt a detailed study, but interested readers are referred to the works listed in the bibliography.

ARVN unit patches were worn as follows; that of the major command to which the soldier belonged (usually a division or higher) was worn on the left sleeve, somewhat lower than American practice. All regimental, battalion and company patches were

Steel-helmeted NVA soldiers pose for a propaganda photo some time in the late 1960s. Three men in the front rank wear the rare 'NVA Combat Jacket' with waistband. The soldier with the improvised netting over his Polish helmet has a rice bag slung at the waist. (Tom Hunt Collection)

worn on the pockets. Generally the higher unit's insignia was worn on the right pocket and the subordinate unit's insignia went on the left. Usually no patches were worn on the right sleeve, except by the Rangers, who invariably wore their star-and-panther Ranger insignia on the left sleeve and used the right for their Corps or Group patch. The National Police Field Force had a system of their own, adapted from their dress uniform. Needless to say, these systems were not always (or even usually) followed, and many ARVN soldiers never bothered wearing patches at all, or perhaps wore the divisional patch alone.

Scarves in bright colours were used by specific units, or to designate subordinate units within larger formations, or as a field sign when different

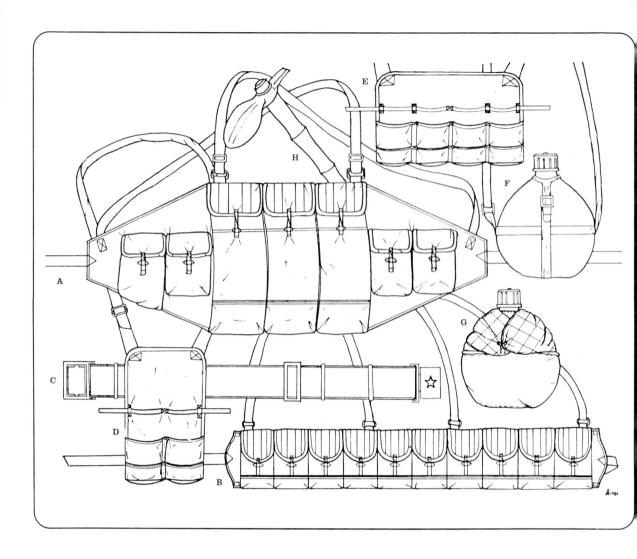

NVA accoutrements: (A) ChiCom AK-47 chest pouch (B) ChiCom SKS chest pouch (C) NVA equipment belt with 'large star' buckle (D) ChiCom two-pocket grenade pouch (E) ChiCom four-pocket grenade pouch (F) Chinese-made 'NVA standard' canteen in web carrier (G) Chinese-made 'VC/early NVA' canteen in carrier (H) VC pick-mattock. (Adapted by permission from 'Vietnam Combat Uniforms', Hunt & Mendez)

types of units worked together on an operation, or (as in the US Army) just to dress up uniforms for a parade or formal inspection. The colours used were commonly scarlet, yellow or bright blue. Camouflage scarves also appeared.

Officers' rank insignia existed in three versions: full colour embroidered, subdued embroidered and metal pin-on types. They could be worn on the cap and both lapels, or a single device would be worn on the shirt. A slip-on type could also be worn on uniforms with shoulder straps. NCO insignia could

appear in the same way, on shoulder straps or on the left sleeve.[1]

ARVN specialist badges (Airborne, Ranger, etc.) also existed as pin-on devices and in cloth embroidered form. They were worn on the right breast above the pocket. Soldiers who had qualified for an American badge wore it above the left pocket. Occasionally a nametape might appear above the right pocket, but this was not especially common. Some 'nametapes', those containing numbers, are actually unit insignia of simple design.

[1]See table of rank insignia, p. 27, MAA 104, *Armies of the Vietnam War 1962–75*.

NVA Uniforms and Insignia

The standard NVA uniform was a dark green cotton shirt and trousers. The shirt had long sleeves, shirt-type cuffs and two pleated button-down pockets closed by pointed flaps. All buttons were of brown plastic. The trousers had only three pockets, two side and one at the right rear. A loop-and-button arrangement permitted the trousers to be gathered at the ankle.

The same uniform was also manufactured in tan-khaki cloth. This was originally an 'export' model, issued to Pathet Lao and Khmer Rouge forces, and NVA units operating alongside them in their countries. Many of these uniforms also found their way into South Vietnam. They were most common in the two southernmost Military Regions. Originally intended for Main Force VC, they were also widely worn by NVA Regulars.

Occasionally NVA soldiers were encountered wearing light blue or grey uniforms. These were NVA Militia items, most commonly seen in the North, often worn by Air Defence crews. Use in the South was extremely rare. Styling was similar to that of other NVA uniforms.

A variety of web belts, with cheap brass or aluminium buckles, were issued to enlisted men. Officers received a version in imitation leather with attached metal buckle.

The NVA soldier received several sets of uniform as his original issue. However, after his arduous transit of the Ho Chi Minh Trail and a few months in the South, he was usually reduced to one, with perhaps a spare shirt or trousers in his pack.

Footwear could be either 'Ho Chi Minh sandals' or the NVA combat shoe. The latter was made in tan canvas with brown rubber lug soles. It was copied from the French Army 'patauga' tropical boot, widely worn by French Union forces during the first Indo-China War.

Standard NVA headgear was the famous sun helmet, sometimes erroneously called a 'pith helmet' by Americans. It was made of a synthetic material called *phenolic*; not a true plastic, this was actually cardboard impregnated with resin under pressure, a process developed in Germany before World War II. During manufacture an outer cloth layer was permanently bonded to the helmet; this was usually dark green in colour, but it was possible to find helmets in tan or brown. A white version is believed to be North Vietnamese Navy issue. In addition to colour, there are two slight variations in style, one being slightly flatter in shape. All versions came with a brown leather chinstrap. Homemade camouflage netting was sometimes added by individual soldiers.

The other common NVA headgear was a floppy bush hat with a cloth chinstrap. It was made in green, tan and brown material, often fading into greys and buffs with wear. Occasionally, tufts of

'Viet Cong Main Force' troops, c.1973. The Viet Cong had virtually ceased to exist as a separate organisation by this date; NVA soldiers filled the ranks of their units, and NVA cadres directed operations. Except for the RPD gunner's M1956 pistol belt and canteen carrier (now doing duty as a pouch) all clothing and equipment seen here are of North Vietnamese origin. (Tom Hunt Collection)

A blurred photo which repays study, of VC Main Force personnel displaying captured ARVN weapons. Most are armed with AK-47s and wear ChiCom chest pouches and US pistol belts. A mixture of black VC and khaki 'NVA Export' uniforms are worn, with bush hats; two men have parachute cloth scarfs. The date is probably the mid-1960s. (US Army)

material were sewn on as camouflage. Some examples of NVA uniform caps also appeared in the South. The issue version, vaguely resembling a World War II Japanese model, was commonly worn in the North as an alternative to the sun helmet when on leave or pass. Cruder versions, similar in style to the US Marine utility cap, were sometimes seen.

Steel helmets were usually worn by anti-aircraft crews, or occasionally by NVA troops in the assault (e.g. the tank-supported attack on the Lang Vei Special Forces Camp). The Polish model was the most common, followed by Czech and East German models. Even old Soviet steel helmets from before World War II were sometimes used. The NVA discarded nothing of value, however slight.

The PAVN had its own system of rank badges for officers and enlisted men. It used collar tabs to indicate both branch and rank; the lack of a branch insignia indicates infantry. An older system used both collar tabs and epaulettes and examples of this type were sometimes found in the South[1]. In general, however, no insignia were worn until very late in the war. Similarly, although both NVA cap and sun helmet made provision for national insignia, this too was rarely worn before the time of the 'Ho Chi Minh Offensive' of 1975. About the only 'insignia' that might be worn by Communist troops before this was a field recognition sign, worn

[1]See table of rank insignia, p. 38, MAA 104, *Armies of the Vietnam War 1962–75.*

by all the troops in one area. This took the form of a single strip of red, yellow or blue cloth tied somewhere on the uniform, the colour changing from day to day. (A special version of this appeared at Hue during the 1968 Tet fighting, featuring short strips of blue and red cloth attached to a white paper square and worn on the arm).

NVA Equipment

The NVA basically used the ChiCom system of accoutrements. Their own guerilla heritage showed through, however, in their wide use of captured, homemade and non-standard items. A description of typical accoutrements follows.

The basis of the Communist soldier's personal equipment was a dark green canvas web equipment belt. There were two main types of belts, both with aluminium buckles and keepers. The centre of the buckle was stamped with a star, and the owner could paint this red, or not, as he chose. To the belt were attached such items as grenade and first-aid pouches, an entrenching tool, and, if one was carried, a knife or machete (usually homemade) in its sheath. All these items slipped on the belt with a simple loop fastening. (The two types of Chinese grenade pouches had a shoulder strap as well.)

Officers received a Sam Browne-type belt in brown imitation leather, with a brass star buckle, supporting a holstered pistol and spare magazine pouch. The shoulder cross strap was rarely worn.

Ammunition was carried in ChiCom chest pouch rigs. These were put on something like a carpenter's apron, by putting the head through the straps and then tying the waist ties behind the back. There was a different type for each weapon.

The chest pouch for the AK-47 (including the Chinese Type 56, etc.) had three 30-round magazine pouches across the chest, flanked by four smaller pockets. Three of these held loose 7.62 × 39 rounds in cardboard boxes, and one held the weapon's combination tool, two-compartment oiler and sometimes a spare firing pin. (Occasionally NVA soldiers used the smaller pouches to carry stick grenades.) A less common carrier was a five-magazine shoulder bag, with external compartments for combination tool, oiler, etc. This also came with an alternative belt loop.

The rig for the SKS (Chinese Type 56) had ten

Soldiers of the 196th Light Inf.Bde., Americal Div., examine a VC cache near Chu Lai in December 1970. The abbreviated rifleman's equipment is typical of short-range operations at this period. Bandoliers are used to carry both magazines and grenades, and spare M-60 belt is looped around the riflemen's waists. The two XM203 grenadiers at the right wear the special grenadier's ammo vest; the man at far right also carries his rifle magazines in a spare canteen carrier, and C-ration toilet paper packs in his helmet band. Third from right has a Kabar knife sheathed in his trouser cargo pocket, and fourth from right has a civilian hunting knife on his belt. (US Army)

individual compartments, nine of which held two 10-round stripper clips of 7.62 × 39 each. A tenth compartment held the oiler. All were closed by peg-and-loop (toggle) fasteners.

The rig for the Moisin-Nagant M1944 bolt-action carbine (Chinese Type 53, often misidentified by GIs as an 'AK-44' or 'K-44') was similar to that for the SKS. Each compartment held three

Lightweight Tropical Rucksack with frame. This consists of a central compartment with drawstring closure, and one large and two small external pockets. The inside of the main compartment flap incorporates a space for stowing maps and papers. Equipment hangers—web loops and webbing with eyelets—appear at the sides of the pack and just above the pockets, though the latter are hidden here by the main flap. The side pockets have a 'tunnel' between their rear face and the side of the main pack, so that items such as machetes can be slipped behind the pockets and attached to the hanger above. The whole pack is made of heavy nylon, and can be strapped to either the top or the bottom of the aluminium tube frame. (US Army)

five-round stripper clips of 7.62 Nagant (a totally different round from that used with the AK and SKS). The compartments were closed by ties rather than toggles.

RPD machine gunners received a round pouch for the weapon's spare drum and its cleaning kit, carried on a shoulder strap.

The NVA used an incredible variety of hand grenades, from factory-manufactured types from China to the crudest jungle workshop copies. They fell into two general categories: cast metal types with striker-release fuses, and stick grenades with wooden handles and pull-friction fuses. All were accommodated by ChiCom pouches, holding two or four grenades each; these slipped on the belt and had a strap to hold the shoulder of the grenade. All NVA grenades were characterised by poor reliability and low explosive power. Metal parts were black or olive, and handles were left natural wood.

In the early days of their involvement the NVA issued a variety of canteens, some in metal, some in plastic. All were of ChiCom manufacture and were the same models used by the Viet Cong. By the late 1960s the NVA had standardised on one canteen: also of Chinese origin, it was of olive-painted aluminium with a brown bakelite cap. It came in a skeleton web carrier, rather like that of the British 1937 web equipment, and was slung over the shoulder on a strap.

The NVA were indefatigable diggers, and their standard shovel closely resembled Soviet or World War II German types. Carrying arrangements were often improvised.

The NVA rucksack was an item unique to Vietnam, its design apparently based on captured French packs of the earlier Indo-China War. It was made of canvas with a large central compartment and three external pockets. The main portion was a bag, closed by means of a drawstring. Its top was covered with a small, squarish flap, secured by two attached straps and their galvanised steel buckles. The three external compartments, the rear one slightly larger than the two at the sides, closed with cloth ties. (Early models of the rucksack were slightly different; among other things, the rear pocket closed with an aluminium buckle.) Adjustable knapsack-type straps attached to the main body. The well-equipped NVA soldier might also have a haversack or 'day-pack' of some type, slung over his shoulder on a strap. NVA troops were issued a green rubberised ground sheet as protection from the elements.

The Plates

A1: Paratrooper, ARVN Airborne Division; Ap Bac, South Vietnam, January 1963
The ARVN paratroops were the first of their Army's élite forces, and saw considerable action

1: Paratrooper, ARVN Airborne Div.; Ap Bac, 1963
2: US Army Captain, advisor to ARVN 2nd Armd.Cav.Regt., 1963
3: US Marine helicopter pilot, 1962-65
4: Nung mercenary, CIDG, 1962-68

A

2

1

3

1: Viet Cong irregular, 1962
2: Viet Cong Main Force soldier, 1964
3: Viet Cong Main Force soldier, 1967

B

1: Staff Sergeant, US 101st Airborne Div., 1965
2: Tank crewman, US 11th Armd.Cav.Regt., 1968
3: SP4 grenadier, US 1st Inf.Div., 1968

C

1, 2: NVA regulars, South Vietnam, 1968
3: NVA anti-aircraft gunner, South Vietnam, 1967

D

1: Lance-Corporal RTO, US 3rd Marine Div., 1965
2: Machine gunner, US Marines; Hue City, Tet 1968
3: Rifleman, 1st Bn., 7th US Marines; MR 1, 1969

E

1: Rifleman, Recce Bn., ROK Capital Div., 1966
2: Helicopter pilot, US Army 1st Aviation Bde., 1970
3: Helicopter crewman, US 1st Air Cavalry Div., 1968

F

1: Enlisted man, RVN National Police Field Force;
   Saigon, Tet 1968
2, 3: ARVN Rangers; Saigon, Tet 1968
4: Marine, RVN 5th Marine Bn., 1972

G

1: LRRP, US 173rd Airborne Bde., 1968
2: US Special Forces, Reconnaissance Team Zeta, 1968
3: US Navy SEAL, Detachment Golf; Rung Sat Special Zone, 1968

during this early period, including combat jumps. One of these took place at the 1963 battle of Ap Bac, when Viet Cong Main Force units inflicted a severe check to ARVN troops and their American advisors.

The ARVN Airborne adopted a camouflage uniform in the early 1960s. In style it resembled the normal fatigues, but with shoulder straps added and all buttons concealed. The camouflage pattern is based on, of all things, the World War II 'windproofs' used by the British SAS, of which surplus stocks were later used, and copied, by French paras in Indo-China. This particular uniform has two pen pockets provided, one under each arm. French paratroop camouflage uniforms in 'lizard' pattern were also worn. Headgear was a cherry red beret or a camouflage fatigue cap, with the Airborne badge on the former. The US M-1C Paratrooper's Steel Helmet was worn in the field. Cloth Vietnamese Basic Parachutist Wings are worn above the right pocket, in the French manner. The insignia on the left pocket is the Jump Status Designator, which indicates that the wearer is currently assigned to an Airborne unit. Rank insignia (*Ha Si*, equivalent to Private First Class) is worn on the left sleeve only, just below the patch of the ARVN Airborne Division (at this time only a brigade). The man's equipment includes a US M1945 Combat Pack (with packstraps improvised from M1945 Belt Suspenders), M1937 BAR Magazine Belt, M1936 Belt Suspenders, M1942 Field Dressing Pouch, and aluminium M1910 Canteen with Carrier. All are US-made and provided under MDAP funds. The soldier is armed with a Browning Automatic Rifle (BAR) in its M1918A2 version. In spite of its 19.4-lb weight it earned many admirers among the ARVN. He also carries US World War II pattern Mk II hand grenades; the ARVN had vast stocks of these and used them throughout the war.

The US M-79 Grenade Carrier Vest, introduced in 1969. (US Army)

A2: US Army Advisor; Ap Bac, January 1963
Despite popular belief, comparatively few of the American advisors to the ARVN were from the Special Forces. Most were ordinary officers and enlisted men. This Army captain, taken from a photograph, is advisor to an ARVN Armored Cavalry unit, its M113 APCs deployed behind him in the rice paddies. He wears the OG 107 Cotton Sateen standard fatigue uniform then coming into service for all branches of the American armed forces. He wears full-colour nametapes, and insignia denoting his branch (Armor) and rank on left and right collar respectively. The tab on his left sleeve identifies him as a graduate of the US Army Ranger School, and the white 'wings' above his left pocket show him to be a qualified paratrooper. Headgear is the despised Army 'baseball cap', on which he wears pin-on metal rank insignia. His private purchase 'tanker boots' are an affectation of US Armor troops. Many American advisors adopted the complete uniform of their Vietnamese units, but this man's only concession to the ARVN is to wear his equivalent Vietnamese rank (*Dai Uy*) on his shirt. He also wears the insignia of the ARVN 2nd Armored Cavalry Regiment in a plastic protective holder suspended from his right shirt pocket. In the early stages of the war advisors were

prohibited from carrying arms, but by this time the .45cal. M1911A1 pistol was common. The M1936 Pistol Belt, two-pocket magazine pouch and M1910 Canteen are World War II models, perhaps the officer's own. His plastic prescription glasses are Army issue, however.

Soldiers of the 1st Inf.Div.'s 61st Inf.Ptn. (Combat Tracker) with one of their Labrador Retriever dogs, near Lai Khe Base Camp, October 1969. Magazines for their CAR-15 SMGs and M-16 rifles are carried in cotton bandoliers and in the newly-issued M1967 Lightweight Ammunition Pouches. Note bag-type 'Two-Quart Canteens' slung from belts, right foreground; and profusion of smoke grenades. This photo shows some of the ways the 'boonie hat' could be worn; and the left hand man wears a locally-made leaf-pattern 'Jones hat'. The sergeant (E5) team leader, sipping from his canteen, wears on his hat a 'Peace Sign' made from a grenade ring and trip-flare wire. The unit's élite status is marked by a shoulder title worn above the 'Big Red One' shoulder patch. (US Army)

Two corporals of the Pathfinder Detachment, 52nd CAB, 1st Aviation Bde. call for extraction after a reconnaissance mission near the Cambodian border, November 1970. Leaf-pattern utilities are worn with both full-colour and subdued unit insignia and nametapes. Airborne and Ranger shoulder titles indicate the unit's élite status. The original print shows metal pin-on rank insignia worn on the shirt collar points. One man uses the AN/PRC-77 radio, successor to the PRC-25, with attached voice scrambling device. By his right hip hang M1944 goggles and an M1942 machete. (US Army)

A3: US Marine helicopter pilot; Project SHUFLY, 1962–65

The Marine Corps made little distinction between the dress of its fixed and rotary wing aircrew, except that helicopter crewmen had to make do with older equipment. This pilot, a Marine captain (all Marine pilots are commissioned officers), wears the standard Navy Bureau of Aeronautics (BuAir) Summer Flying Coveralls and brown leather flying boots. The grey leather gloves are also Navy pilot's issue. His APH-6A Pilot's Protective Helmet is a

standard model adapted for use with a helicopter's communications system. Even older helmets were worn. It has been hurriedly overpainted Olive Drab to reduce visibility. The pilot carries a .38 calibre Smith & Wesson Model 10 revolver for personal defence.

A4: Nung mercenary, Civilian Irregular Defense Group (CIDG); 1962–68

The CIDG Programme was an early American attempt to harness the military potential of ethnic minorities within Vietnam on the side of the GVN (Government of Vietnam), which denied them membership in the armed forces.

The United States provided several types of camouflage clothing to the Vietnamese. This man wears a mixture of two. His 'tiger-stripe' uniform is an ERDL-type (see main text), recognisable by the 'cigarette pocket' on the left trouser leg (its actual purpose was to hold a field dressing.) The Vietnamese were soon producing copies of this uniform; the ARVN Rangers in particular affected this particular style, with its exposed two-button pockets. The CIDG's cap is an American commercial pattern (intended for waterfowl hunters) styled after the US Marine utility cap. An all-round-brim style (sometimes called a 'Jones hat') was also popular, and could be worn in various ways, often in a 'cowboy' style—the Vietnamese were fascinated by American Western movies. The black silk scarf identifies an ethnic Chinese Nung unit. Each of the minority groups participating in the CIDG programme had its own colours.

In addition to serving in their own units, a Nung platoon served with each Special Forces Camp as a security detachment. Being of Chinese descent, their ancient racial prejudices made them invulnerable to infiltration by the Viet Cong. Their pay was provided for by the SF soldiers themselves, out of their own pockets.

At this stage of the war personal equipment was minimal, and here comprises M1956 Pistol Belt, Suspenders, Universal Pouch and Canteen. The CIDG tended to have M1956 equipment, while the ARVN itself had the older World War II/Korean War type. The M-2 carbine carried by this man was extremely popular among Oriental soldiers, due to its small size, light weight and fully automatic capability. Vietnamese-made copies of the French

A much-reprinted photo of VC Main Force troops in about 1964. They wear tan-khaki uniforms, and Chinese-made sun helmets with foliage netting—a cloth cover was far more common. Their AK magazines are carried in the early five-pocket shoulder bag. (Tom Hunt Collection)

'patauga' jungle boot are worn. In 1969 all CIDG units were incorporated in the ARVN proper, either as Ranger Border Defense Battalions or as Regional or Popular Force units.

B1: Viet Cong irregular, 1962

This man, a local guerilla, wears a mixture of civilian dress and old French items, with homemade accoutrements and the very beginnings of North Vietnamese aid. His clothing is the famous 'black pyjama' peasant dress of Vietnam: a collarless shirt, here with three open pockets, and elastic-waisted trousers. Footwear is the 'Ho Chi Minh sandal', a surprisingly efficient item made from old truck tyres and inner tubes; and he wears an old French Army bush hat. His canvas equipment belt has an excellent copy of a US buckle. Accoutrements include a homemade haversack and grenade pouch, the latter fabricated from bright green commercial tent cloth; it holds two 'jungle workshop' fragmentation grenades of different types. A knife, handmade from an old US file, is stuck through the belt. The black cotton rice bag, worn around the body, is said to hold a month's supply of grain (often infested with vermin). His weapon is an old French bolt-action MAS-36 in calibre 7.5 × 54mm, typical of those stored away by the Viet

Minh for future use at the end of the Indo-China War. Fifty rounds of its ammunition are carried in the homemade bandolier; the cloth and buttons for this item come from an old shirt. Out of sight on the man's left hip is a Chinese-made canteen in a canvas carrier, provided by North Vietnam.

B2: Viet Cong Main Force soldier, 1964

His 'black pyjamas' could be of the civilian type or the VC pattern, which was a simplified version of the North Vietnamese Army uniform shirt and trousers. His headgear is a Chinese-manufactured plastic sun helmet covered with waterproof nylon material. Around his neck he wears a scarf of US parachute cloth. His rice bag is carried around his neck. Accoutrements are a mixture of NVA, Chinese and 'jungle workshop' items. His equipment belt is NVA issue, and supports a ChiCom two-pocket grenade pouch and canteen. Hand grenades are of Chinese manufacture, copies of World War II Japanese models. The Chinese have also provided the 7.62mm Type 53 carbine (a copy of the Soviet M1944) and its ten-pocket ammunition pouch rig. The pack is a local item, made from US nylon rain poncho material, with one large and one small compartment and two side pockets. The pick-mattock entrenching tool is also a local item, with a bamboo handle and hand-forged iron head. It is attached to the belt by means of a strip of inner tube. Ho Chi Minh sandals complete the soldier's combat dress.

B3: Viet Cong Main Force soldier, 1967

This *linh tron* (rifleman) wears the NVA 'export' khaki uniform and bush hat. Accoutrements comprise a ChiCom chest pouch rig for the SKS, NVA equipment belt, ChiCom two-pocket grenade pouch, a first-aid (or medical) pouch and a Chinese canteen in a canvas carrier. His NVA rucksack is camouflaged by means of branches inserted through a ring device (see Plate D2). Ho Chi Minh sandals are worn. A ChiCom Type 56 rifle is carried, distinguished by the characteristic spike bayonet. The stick-type fragmentation grenades are also of Chinese origin.

Two Viet Cong prisoners taken by the 101st Airborne Div. in 1966 display the two main types of 'black pyjama' shirts: the collarless civilian type (left) and the VC uniform type (right). (US Army)

C1: US Army Staff Sergeant, 101st Airborne Division, 1965

The 101st was among the first major units to deploy to Vietnam, and the sergeant's appearance is typical of this period. His M-1 steel helmet is covered with a reversible camouflage cover held in place by an elastic camouflage band; the band also holds a plastic bottle of insect repellent. He wears the early model jungle uniform, with exposed buttons and full-colour insignia and nametapes. His newly procured jungle boots are the early pattern, without ankle reinforcement. The light blue infantry branch scarf (actually an ascot) is a component of the Class A Service Uniform; it was briefly worn in the field during the early period (very briefly—nylon is hot!) The sergeant's equipment is the M1956 set, comprising Pistol Belt, Belt Suspenders, Field Pack, two Universal Pouches and three OD Plastic Canteens in carriers. His First Aid Dressing Pouch is attached to his suspenders on the right side, and an Army issue angle-head flashlight is attached to one ammo pouch. His entrenching tool in its M-56 Carrier also incorporates provision for the M-7 Bayonet in Scabbard M8A1 as shown. The metal snap ring attached to the left side of his harness is used in rappelling from helicopters and is thus a distinction of Airborne and Air Cavalry

Miscellaneous clothing, equipment and personal effects of the NVA soldier. (Tom Hunt Collection)

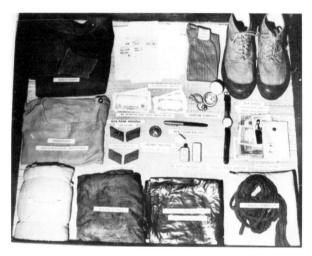

troopers. His weapon is the newly issued M-16, the early model with three-prong flash suppressor. At this stage of the war, its issue was limited to Airborne and Air Cavalry units.

C2: US Army tank crewman, 11th Armored Cavalry Regiment, 1968

Armour crewmen in Vietnam wore the same uniforms as everyone else. Personal equipment was dictated by the nature of their duties. Poor visibility from inside the vehicles often required the crews to expose heads and upper torsos during operations, so flak vests were common wear (ordinarily these were worn by Army troops only in static positions). This man has the later version of the Army M1952, without shoulder straps and with a three-quarter

collar added. Although steel helmets were preferred, the vehicle's communications system required some personnel to wear the CVC (Combat Vehicle Crewman's) helmet, made of fibreglass and offering little protection from enemy fire. The M1944 goggles worn with it were also issued to drivers of ordinary wheeled vehicles. As personal protection this man carries a .45 pistol in a shoulder holster. Other weapons (rifle, sub-machine gun or grenades) were usually kept within reach. Because of the carrying capacity of the vehicles, tank and mechanised troops enjoyed a relatively higher standard of living than other troops—all without the need to carry a rucksack. On the other hand, their vehicles were prime targets wherever they went. This man wears no insignia at all on his uniform, a practice in some units, depending on the operation. He is currently examining the contents of a captured NVA rucksack, which include an NVA 'export' tan shirt (widely used by the Viet Cong) and one variety of issue ricebowl.

C3: US Army Sp4 grenadier, 1st Infantry Division, 1968
This soldier wears the later-style utilities (made in rip-stop cotton) with an OD towel as a sweat rag. His M-56 equipment has some additions reflecting his duties as a grenadier. The M-79 40mm Grenade Launcher was a new type of infantry weapon and its ammunition was originally issued in special cotton bandoliers, each holding six rounds in two 'packs' of three (each 'pack' further secured in a plastic holder). The original issue of two bandoliers proved totally inadequate, and further rounds were carried in ammo pouches and empty Claymore mine bags. This soldier also carries one M-18 Colored Smoke Grenade, used for signalling purposes. They were made in red, green, yellow and violet, and the colour of the smoke was indicated by the top of the grenade and also by the markings. The soldier carries the Lightweight Tropical Rucksack, which had replaced the M1956 Combat Pack in most infantry units by this time. Attached to its aluminium frame are a rolled nylon poncho and poncho liner (used in lieu of a sleeping bag in the field) and four OD Plastic Canteens slung on a nylon cord, supplementing two worn in normal fashion on the belt. An M1942 Machete in its sheath is slipped through a tunnel behind one pocket of the rucksack. In the camouflage band of his helmet this

soldier carries several packs of C-Ration matches and a locally-made plastic cigarette case. He also wears an Ace-of-Spades playing card, used by some units to advertise their presence throughout their AO (Area of Operations). He holds a captured ChiCom Type 56 LMG, a copy of the Soviet RPD; this was the standard NVA and VC Main Force LMG by this period. Its spare drum carrier lies at the entrance to the tunnel, alongside a Chinese copy of the Soviet ShM-1 gas mask.

The NVA sun helmet. (Tom Hunt Collection)

D1: NVA Regular, South Vietnam, 1968

This NVA rifleman wears the standard North Vietnamese uniform of dark green shirt and trousers, together with canvas and rubber combat shoes. Headgear is the characteristic NVA sun helmet. No insignia is worn in the South. He is armed with a Chinese Type 56 assault rifle; this differs from the Soviet AK-47 in providing a triangular bayonet. Ammunition and magazines are carried in a ChiCom chest pouch. Attached to his equipment belt is a ChiCom four-pocket grenade pouch with Chinese-made stick grenades. He also wears an NVA rucksack, and a Czechoslovakian-made haversack, or 'day-pack', on his left hip. A Chinese-made canteen is slung over one shoulder, out of sight. The yellow cloth worn around the neck is an NVA field sign; the colour changed daily. The activities of American Recon and Special Forces made such precautions necessary by this stage of the war. The background is an NVA base camp, typical of Laos or the sanctuaries of the Cambodian border. Facilities there could be quite elaborate.

D2: NVA Regular, South Vietnam, 1968

The NVA considered the RPG launcher a crew-served weapon and issued it to three-man teams. This man is the actual gunner. In addition to his RPG-2, he carries an SKS rifle (his two assistants would have AK-47s.) In place of a sun helmet he wears the alternative NVA bush hat. His trousers are gathered at the ankles by a loop-and-button arrangement. The rocket pack is a jungle workshop item, with provision for four RPG rounds and their booster charges on the flap, and spare clothing, etc., within. The standard ChiCom rocket pack was also used, but most RPG teams simply carried their rockets in bags or baskets, or stuffed them 'pointy-

end first' into rucksack pockets and tied up the loose ends with string. On his equipment belt this soldier wears a green leather cartridge box for his rifle ammunition, and a homemade knife in a sheath. His canteen is the standard NVA model, of ChiCom manufacture. Tucked under the flap of his pack is his folded jungle hammock and groundsheet. The ring device tied to the top is an NVA camouflage holder; branches and foliage were slipped through the rings on the march. This soldier has elected to wear his 'colour of the day' as an armband pinned to his sleeve.

D3: NVA anti-aircraft gunner, South Vietnam, 1967

This figure is based on descriptions of NVA anti-aircraft troops taken prisoner by the 173rd Airborne Brigade after the battle of Dak To in late 1967. He is dressed in the blue cotton NVA Militia uniform, common issue in the North, but a rarity in South Vietnam; its cut exactly follows that of other NVA uniforms. His belt, with aluminium buckle, is standard NVA issue for enlisted men; and his steel helmet is of Polish origin, the most commonly seen type. Footwear is the Ho Chi Minh sandal, also widely used by the NVA. As his duties will keep him close to a base camp, he does not need to wear a field sign. He holds an issue of *Quyet Tien*, the NVA Army newspaper, one of several publications distributed among NVA troops in the South.

E1: US Marine radioman; Operation STARLITE, August 1965

Operation STARLITE, conducted against the 1st VC Regiment in the 'Street Without Joy' region of I Corps, was the first major Marine operation of the war. This lance-corporal's uniform and equip-

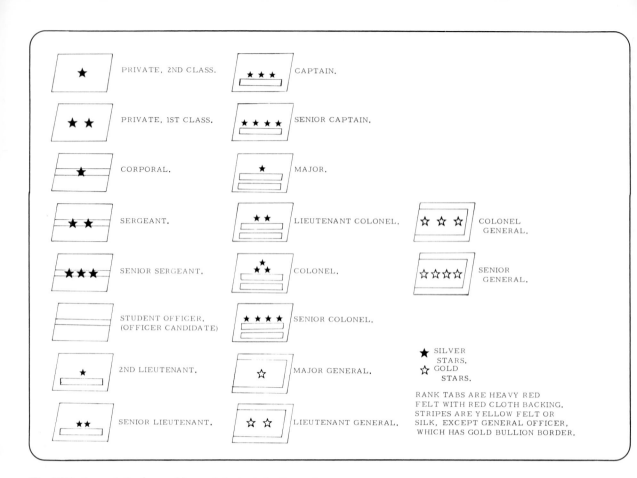

★	PRIVATE, 2ND CLASS.	★★★	CAPTAIN.	
★★	PRIVATE, 1ST CLASS.	★★★★	SENIOR CAPTAIN.	
★	CORPORAL.	★	MAJOR.	
★★	SERGEANT.	★★	LIEUTENANT COLONEL.	☆ ☆ ☆ COLONEL GENERAL.
★★★	SENIOR SERGEANT.	★★	COLONEL.	☆☆☆☆ SENIOR GENERAL.
	STUDENT OFFICER. (OFFICER CANDIDATE)	★★★★	SENIOR COLONEL.	
★	2ND LIEUTENANT.	☆	MAJOR GENERAL.	★ SILVER STARS. ☆ GOLD STARS.
★★	SENIOR LIEUTENANT.	☆ ☆	LIEUTENANT GENERAL.	RANK TABS ARE HEAVY RED FELT WITH RED CLOTH BACKING. STRIPES ARE YELLOW FELT OR SILK, EXCEPT GENERAL OFFICER, WHICH HAS GOLD BULLION BORDER.

The NVA changed the form of its rank insignia in the early 1960s from the collar tab and shoulder strap sequence illustrated on p. 38 of MAA 104, *Armies of the Vietnam War 1962–75,* **to the collar-only sequence illustrated here; Allied intelligence never bothered to update their identification chart, and to the author's knowledge this is the first time the correct insignia have been published. (M. Albert Mendez)**

ment are typical of the period. He wears the Marine HBT utilities, of 1950s vintage, and the characteristic Marine utility cap. The Marine globe-and-anchor insignia is stencilled on both. Rank insignia are displayed as metal pin-on devices on both shirt lapels. In common with most US troops at this time, he has yet to receive jungle boots and so wears his black leather issue. His reversible helmet camouflage cover is worn 'brown side out' in the coastal sand dunes; a camouflage band has been improvised from a strip of inner tube. His personal equipment includes the M1961 Rifle Belt and Ammunition Pouches, especially designed for the M-14 rifle. The rest of his equipment is of much older vintage. The Belt Suspenders and Jungle First Aid Kit (worn at the rear of the belt) are World War II models, as is the Three-Pocket Grenade

Pouch. Also out of sight is an aluminium M1910 Canteen and carrier, worn at the left rear of the belt. An M-6 Bayonet in Scabbard M-8A1 is attached to the bottom of one ammunition pouch. The AN/PRC-10 radio is an obsolescent model dating from the Korean War, but still in use by the Marines. Although it has its own harness, it was usually carried as shown, lashed to a fibre pack-board. It is marked with the insignia of the 3rd Marine Division. Due to the weight of his equipment, this man has chosen not to wear his flak vest. Booby-traps and North Vietnamese artillery will soon deny him this option. His personal weapon is the 7.62mm M-14 rifle in its standard version; variants existed, and the weapon was extensively used by the Army as well. Due to initial problems with the M-16, the older rifle remained the weapon of choice for many Marines until late in the war.

E2: US Marine machine gunner; Hue City, Tet Offensive, February 1968

Adapted from a photograph, this Marine M-60 gunner wears an intermediate type of jungle utilities with concealed buttons. Over this he wears a nylon US Navy Rain Jacket, and the Marine M1955 Armor Vest. His personal equipment includes the Marine Jungle First Aid Kit and two OD Plastic Canteens in M1910 Carriers. As a machine gunner he is also issued a .45 pistol and a Kabar knife in lieu of a bayonet. All of these are attached directly to the bottom of the vest, which has a row of grommets around the bottom for this purpose. The Kabar's sheath is inserted behind the M1916 Holster (an old brown one dyed black). His steel helmet has the older pattern World War II/Korea camouflage cover. The improvised camouflage band holds a can of LSA (Lubricant, Small Arms) and a toothbrush used to clean the weapon. The man's personal possessions are carried in the Marine Haversack, made up as a Light Marching Pack.

It makes provision for an M1943 Entrenching Tool in carrier on the flap. Beneath the flap itself is a folded nylon rain poncho also used by the Army. Extra ammunition for the M-60 is carried in several ways. One belt is worn bandolier fashion and a second is carried in a cardboard box with its own strap. Additional belts would be carried in metal

ARVN 22nd Div. soldiers board a UH-1D helicopter of 189th Assault Support Helicopter Company—'Ghostriders'—in November 1970. The Central Highlands could be chilly in certain seasons, as indicated by the American crewman's M1951 Field Jacket and the closed doors of the Huey. The ARVN troopers wear tightly-tailored copies of the American OG 107 fatigues, and M-56 equipment; the arrangement of the latter with two ammo pouches at the front, two at the back and the canteens on the hips was characteristic of the ARVN. Two-pocket rucksacks are worn with MG belts, LAWs, entrenching tools, bayonets, Claymore bags, etc., tied on as securely as possible. One man has his squad's rice cooking pot tied up in waterproof nylon. 'Assault' slings have been improvised for the M-16s from the standard issue. (US Army)

ammunition cans. M-60 belts were loaded one-in-five with tracer bullets, but individual unit SOPs (Standard Operating Procedures) could alter this.

E3: US Marine rifleman, 1st Battalion, 7th Marines; MR 1, spring 1969

Starting in late 1968, the new 'Leaf-Pattern' Camouflage Uniform was adopted by the Marine Corps. Unlike the Army, the Marines were allowed to 'mix and match' camouflage with regular jungle utilities during the transition period. This rifleman has the modified M1955 Armor Vest, with two crude pockets sewn on the front. He is equipped only for a short patrol. M-16 magazines are carried in a bandolier and an old Claymore bag, and the pockets of the vest. M1910 Canteen Carriers were becoming scarce by this time, but this man has found one to carry an OD Plastic Canteen. His Jungle First Aid Kit, attached at the rear of his flak vest, is not visible from this angle. Graffiti on helmets and flak vests were common, but this man has only his name and serial number, as required by unit orders. His helmet camouflage band is used to hold several packets of C-Ration toilet paper against future need. His M-16A1 Rifle is the later model with 'birdcage' flash suppressor and bolt assist on the right side of the receiver.

F1: Private, Reconnaissance Battalion, ROK Capital ('Tiger') Division, 1966

Unlike some other armies, the Republic of Korea provided uniforms and equipment for its Vietnam contingent. This man wears a Korean-made camouflage suit, originally procured by the ROK Marine Corps, but also used by the Army and Special Forces. Its style is a simplified version of the USMC utilities shown in Plate E1. Korean-made combat boots are worn, although the ROK forces were quick to obtain US and ARVN jungle boots. The helmet is the World War II version of the M-1; its liner has its own leather chinstrap, in addition to the canvas strap of the helmet shell. Black electrical tape holds the ROK camouflage cover in place. Regulations for wear of the divisional shoulder patch were vague and placement could follow US or ARVN practice. Personal equipment is the US Korean War pattern, with M1945 Combat Pack and Suspenders, OD Plastic Canteen in M1910 Carrier, and the M1936 Cartridge Belt issued to

1/9 Cavalry reconnaissance troopers, November 1970. The left hand man wears a 'tiger-stripe' beret over a camouflage bandage worn as a headscarf, and a ChiCom chest pouch for his captured folding-stock AK-47. Piled at their feet are a Lightweight Rucksack, a mesh M-79 Grenadier's Vest, and an AN/PRC-25 radio awaiting insertion into a rucksack. The aircraft shelter is made of PSP, a universal engineering material in Vietnam. (US Army)

personnel armed with the M-1 Garand rifle. M1956-type web gear came into use soon after arrival in Vietnam.

F2: US Army helicopter pilot, 1st Aviation Brigade, 1970

This Army captain, returning from a decoration ceremony, wears the two-piece flying suit ('Shirt and Trousers, Flyer's, Hot Weather, Fire Resistant Nylon OG 106'). Especially developed for Army aviators, it was made of Nomex, a fire-resistant synthetic, and was first issued in late 1969. Sleeves were tightly tailored to discourage personnel from rolling them up (some did anyway), and it included a multiplicity of pockets. Most of the insignia worn here are of subdued pattern, as per regulation. These include the pilot's nametapes, branch (infantry) and rank insignia, and the Army Aviator's Badge above the left pocket. Full-colour insignia (reserved for 'best dress') include the shoulder patch of the 1st Aviation Brigade (left shoulder), the 121st Aviation Company on the left pocket, and this unit's RAZORBACKS platoon patch on the right. The last two items are examples of unofficial unit insignia. The man also wears the full-colour patch of the 4th Infantry Division on his right sleeve, indicating a previous combat tour with that unit.

His black Stetson hat is an affectation of some Cavalry and Aviation units in the early 1970s; it was strictly for ceremonial purposes, and was not worn in the field, as some film-makers would have us believe. His personal weapon is a .45cal. M1911 pistol in a locally-made leather holster and gunbelt. Jungle boots are worn, although some aircrew preferred leather ones. Sunglasses are Army Aviation issue. The decoration is the Silver Star medal, the third highest American medal, awarded 'For Gallantry in Action' against the armed enemies of the United States.

F3: US Army helicopter crewman, 1st Cavalry Division (Airmobile), 1968
Before the introduction of Nomex uniforms, Army helicopter crews flew in standard fatigues. Ordinary ground troops' body armour was worn. In late 1968 the Army introduced new types especially for aircrews. This man, an Sp5 crew chief of the 229th Assault Helicopter Battalion, wears the version for gunners and crew chiefs. Usually called the 'chickenplate vest', it comprised front and back plates of aluminium oxide ceramic armour, moderately effective against high-velocity small arms projectiles. A version for helicopter pilots and co-pilots (who had armoured seats to sit in) comprised only the front plate. Later models used lighter and stronger ceramics which reduced the weight slightly from this model's 25lbs. The crew chief also wears the Army APH-5A Flyer's Helmet with integral headphones and boom mike. His weapon is the famous 'Swedish K' (Kulsprutpistole M45 'Carl Gustav'), a 9mm weapon originally introduced into Vietnam in the early 1960s by the CIA. The Sp5's moustache is a typical indulgence, and not only of Aviation units. His sunglasses are Army issue for aircrews.

G1: Policeman, RVN National Police Field Force; Saigon, Tet Offensive, February 1968
This man wears the distinctive 'leopard' camouflage uniform of his organisation. Its style is the most common one for Vietnamese camouflage uniforms, similar to the standard fatigues but with added pockets on the trouser legs. His sleeves are cut short and sewn to simulate rolled-up sleeves. Insignia placement is unusual, but taken from photographs. On his right sleeve he wears the

subdued patch of the 500th National Police Field Force Company, and on his left that of the Capital Special Zone. (Most NPFFs wore no insignia, or sometimes just their Company patch suspended in a holder from the right pocket.) His armour vest is a special version of the US M1952 made expressly for the ARVN in small sizes, and differing from its US counterpart in having Velcro closures for the pockets and front fly. His web gear includes two locally-manufactured pouches for his M-3 submachine gun. Although he wears a US helmet here, normal headgear would be a black beret with a silver badge.

G2: ARVN Ranger; Saigon, Tet Offensive February 1968
In the mid-1960s, the ARVN Rangers adopted a leaf-pattern camouflage uniform to replace earlier types. It was also worn by other ARVN élite forces. For more general details, see below.

G3: ARVN Ranger; Saigon, Tet Offensive, February 1968
Early-war ARVN Rangers wore standard utilities. Camouflage clothing was generally a 'tiger-stripe' variant, but other types were also seen, and one of these is shown here. It is of American ERDL origin, one of several patterns procured for the GVN in the early 1960s. (The Vietnamese later produced their

Viet Cong pose for a propaganda photo with AK-47 and RPG-2; the RPG gunner carries extra rockets and booster charges in a 'jungle workshop' rocket pack. He wears 'black pyjama' clothing, and his assistant seems to have a civilian shirt. Note the characteristic floppy, low-crowned bush hats. (US Army)

own copies.) Americans generally called this type of camouflage the 'duck hunter pattern'. There were variations in colour and styling. The primary user was supposed to be the CIDG, but examples found their way to other units.

The ARVN Rangers distinguished themselves by a flamboyant display of bright colours and insignia, even on combat clothing. The Ranger shoulder patch was inevitably displayed on the left arm, and occasionally a Corps patch—a red Roman numeral on a white disc—appeared on the right. Battalion and commemorative patches were worn on the pockets. In the early 1970s a complicated system of coloured shoulder tabs distinguished different Ranger Groups. Prior to this, US or Vietnamese Ranger tabs were worn. One Vietnamese version is shown here (as always, there were variants!), bearing the words *Biet Dong Quan* (Ranger). Brightly coloured scarves in company colours were common. A maroon beret with the Ranger badge was also worn (the Airborne-qualified 91st Rangers had red berets instead). In the field, helmets were painted in camouflage colours and prominently marked with the Ranger star-and-black-panther insignia.

This soldier, fighting in Saigon during the 1968 Tet Offensive, wears an improvised ammo vest over his uniform, made from an old fatigue shirt. He carries further magazines in a bandolier tied around his waist. His weapon is the A1 version of the M-16, which the ARVN began to receive in large numbers about this time. He wears ARVN 'Goalong' jungle boots, which were used along with American types.

G4: Marine, RVN 5th Marine Battalion, 1972
The field uniform of the Vietnamese Marine Corps was another example of the ubiquitous 'tiger-stripes'. The pocket style is typical of the VNMC. The shoulder patch is that of the Vietnamese Marine Corps as a whole; individual battalions were distinguished by the background colour of the nametape (for the 5th, white lettering on blue tape). Such decorations were usually omitted in the field. Formal headgear was a green beret with metal VNMC globe-and-anchor device; in the field, either a 'tiger-stripe' utility cap or 'Jones hat' was worn. The same material was also used for helmet covers, as shown. The weapon is an American M-72 LAW (Light Anti-tank Weapon), a disposable rocket launcher. The man also carries M-59

A US Marine helicopter pilot holds the remains of his survival radio, smashed by two enemy bullets during a mission in 1969. He wears the US Navy CS/FRP-1 flying suit ('Coveralls, Flying Summer, Fire-Resistant, Polyamide') with a black leather namepatch on the left breast. This suit replaced the earlier cotton type shown in the colour plates during the mid-1960s and was standard issue for all Navy and Marine fixed-wing and helicopter aircrew thereafter. A Marine major's oakleaf is pinned to the utility cap; personal equipment includes a .45 pistol and a Pilot's Survival Knife worn on an M1936 Pistol Belt, recognisable by its metal snap. (USMC)

'baseball' hand grenades, smaller and easier to throw than the M-26.

H1: US Army LRRP, 74th Infantry Detachment (Airborne) (LRRP), 173rd Airborne Brigade, 1968
In all the long history of America's wars, there was never anything like the LRRPs, the Army's élite Long Range Reconnaissance Patrols. Infiltrated in five-man teams into enemy territory, their mission was the location of targets for the Air Force and artillery. They also carried out raids and sabotage against enemy base camps and lines of communications, but their primary purpose remained observation, not combat. However, if cornered, a LRRP Team usually had enough firepower and

combat experience to defeat much larger NVA units and hold off reinforcements until they could be extracted.

This man wears the ARVN camouflage beret, which along with the camouflage 'Jones hat' and M1951 Patrol Cap was the usual combat headgear of all Allied élite forces. 'Leaf-pattern' camouflage utilities are worn with M1956 Pistol Belt and Suspenders and four Universal Pouches. These held a total of 16 M-16 magazines, and a further 14 were often carried in two bandoliers tied around the waist. At 19 rounds per magazine (a full 20 might cause malfunction) this gave a total of 570 rounds for the weapon—in this case an XM-177, universally known as a CAR-15. This was the SMG version of the M-16. Four OD Plastic Canteens in M1967 Carriers are worn on the belt, and four more are attached to the Lightweight Tropical Rucksack frame. (A large amount of water was needed for the special freeze-dried LRRP rations, and the NVA would normally control all sources of fresh water in the vicinity.) Carried on the rucksack were a poncho and liner, 15 feet of rope and Claymore mines. (Two men per team also had AN/PRC-25 radios.)

Several types of grenades are carried. An M-26A1 Fragmentation Grenade is attached to the harness, and taped together around one Universal Pouch are an M-34 'Willie Peter' (White Phosphorus) and an M-18 Colored Smoke Grenade. Ten further 'frags', four more WP and several different M-18s went into Rucksack pockets or empty Claymore bags. A private purchase Randall Model 14 Attack Knife is carried in a custom leg sheath. Other items carried might include explosives and demo cord, special electronics gear, etc.

Korean officers and enlisted men of the ROK Capital ('Tiger') Division on arrival at Nha Trang Airport, October 1965. Both plain and camouflage uniforms are in evidence, both being patterned in imitation of 1950s USMC utilities. The helmet covers are made from Korean camouflage material. Packs and accoutrements are US World War II patterns, with standard US M-17A1 Protective Masks in carriers worn slung on the left hip. The four nearest officers display an interesting collection of Field Dressing Pouches—M1942 and M1910 models, and a leather type usually issued to Military Police. Bedrolls are correctly fastened around the outside edges of M1945 Combat Packs. (US Army)

*H2: Staff Sergeant, US Army Special Forces, RT Zeta,
MACV-SOG, 1968*

Reconnaisance Team Zeta was one of a number of
similar teams conducting covert cross-border oper-

**Members of a US Navy SEAL unit climb aboard a STAB ('SEAL
Team Assault Boat') to begin a combat mission in late 1968.
Uniforms are a mixture of 'tiger-stripes' and 'leaf-pattern'
utilities, but the shotgunner and radioman wear instead the
SEAL Rifleman's Jacket. Headgear includes a beret and 'Jones
hats' in 'tiger-stripes' and a standard OD 'boonie hat'. Minimal
accoutrements are worn. The radioman has a flotation
bladder below his radio; note also the bending of the antenna
under the set for convenience and concealment—this did not
affect the radio's performance. The bag at the side of the radio
holds the long-range antenna. The SEAL at left, the inspiration
for Plate H3, carries the commercial Ithaca Model 37 shotgun;
changes in American hunting laws in the early 1960s created a
market for short-barrelled shotguns for deer hunting, and a
wide range of these were purchased by various government
agencies for use in Vietnam, where they supplemented older
patterns of riot gun in the inventory. Another weapons note: at
far right, see the pintle-mounted M-60 with a standard field
modification seen on helicopter, boat and vehicle mountings
where the gun would be fired by one man without a loader: a C-
ration can brazed below the feedway! (US Navy)**

ations under the auspices of the Military Assistance
Command Vietnam's Studies and Observation
Group (MACV-SOG). It operated in the tri-
border region of Laos, Cambodia and Vietnam
under the direction of Command and Control
Central (CCC), based at Kontum, RVN. A
mixture of indigenous personnel and American
Special Forces were employed. This SF trooper
wears a private-purchase 'tiger-stripe' camouflage
uniform; this version is a Thai pattern, and was
probably obtained on a Bangkok R&R. Headgear
is an ARVN camouflaged 'Jones hat' with brim
removed.

As load-bearing equipment this man wears a
STABO rig, manufactured at the unit level from
nylon aircraft harness. It doubled as an extraction
harness. Attached are an Air Force strobe light in its
case and a PAL RH-36 Knife. The standard M1956

Pistol Belt, worn as part of the harness, holds four M1956 Universal Pouches and two Two-Quart Canteens. The Pack is an ARVN two-pocket rucksack with integral 'X'-frame. This was preferred by many SF and Recon personnel because it allowed items to be worn at the back of the belt. (The frame of the Lightweight Tropical Rucksack prevented this.) The rucksack holds an AN/PRC-25 Radio with a plastic bag fastened around the handset to keep moisture away from components. Two M-26A1 Fragmentation Grenades are ready for instant use at the belt; additional grenades are carried in two Claymore bags slung over the rucksack, and two standard canteens are attached at the sides. The weapon is an M-16 fitted with a Human Engineering Laboratories M-4 Silencer and an AN/PVS-2 Starlite Scope. Reconnaissance Teams were individually configured for specific missions (some of unusual nature) and the special equipment carried varied with each.

H3: US Navy SEAL, Detachment Golf, SEAL Team ONE; Rung Sat Special Zone, 1968

The Navy SEAL Detachments were small, specialised units charged with conducting Special Warfare operations in a maritime environment. Their members were UDT qualified personnel ('frogmen') who had received extensive training in unconventional warfare techniques. Five Detachments of SEALs operated in Vietnam under control of the Commander, Naval Forces, Vietnam (COMNAVFORV). They engaged in several types of missions, mostly intelligence collection, raids and ambushes. They were also used to recover sensitive material from crashed aircraft, and for diving operations of various types. Some of these activities were apparently carried out in North Vietnam. Detachment Golf, however, had its AO in the nightmare wilderness of the Rung Sat Special Zone, just off the main shipping channel to Saigon—easily the worst terrain in the whole of Vietnam.

This SEAL is lightly armed for his overnight mission, perhaps to ambush a Viet Cong courier. His Remington 870 shotgun was one of a number of civilian types procured for RVN use. He wears an unusual 'leaf-pattern' camouflage jacket, designed especially for the SEALs: it incorporated pockets for M-16 magazines, and an internal flotation bladder.

This is the rifleman's model; versions for XM203 grenadiers and radiomen also existed. Very few of these garments were apparently produced. His hat is the OD 'boonie hat', first introduced in 1967. Sometimes sneaker-type 'coral shoes' were worn instead of jungle boots.

Select Bibliography

Uniforms and insignia:

Hunt, Thomas J. & Mendez, M. Albert, *Vietnam Combat Uniforms*, Gateway Hobbies, 62 W. 38th St, NY 10018, 1980.

Lulling, Darrel R., *Communist Militaria of the Vietnam War (Revised Edition)*, MCN Press, Tulsa, OK 74105, 1980.

Smyth, Cecil B. Jr., *Army of the Republic of Vietnam, Infantry Insignia*,

Smyth, Cecil B. Jr., *Army of the Republic of Vietnam, Territorial Forces Insignia*,

Smyth, Cecil B. Jr., *Army of the Republic of Vietnam, Ranger Insignia*, all ARV-CAT, P.O. Box 3102, Virginia Beach, VA, 1976

The Vietnam War:

Lewy, Guenter, *America in Vietnam*, Oxford University Press, NY, 1978.

Palmer, Dave Richard, *Summons of the Trumpet, U.S.-Vietnam in Perspective*, Presidio Press, San Rafael, CA, 1978.

Summers, Harry G. Jr., *On Strategy, The Vietnam War in Context*, Superintendent of Documents, US government Printing Office, Washington, DC 20402, 1981.

Westmoreland, William C., *A Soldier Reports*, Doubleday & Co., Garden City, NY, 1976.

The author also recommends the excellent US Army *Vietnam Studies* monographs, available from the US Government Printing Office, Washington DC; and the publications of the History and Museums Division, Headquarters, US Marine Corps, Washington DC.

INDEX

(References to illustrations are shown in **bold**. Plates are shown with page and caption locators in brackets.)

ammunition 9, 9–10, 10
Ap Bac, battle of, 1963: 25
ARVN 12, 17–18, 18–19, **33**
   equipment 10, **11**, **A1** (25), 28, **33**
   headgear 5, **11**, **13**, **15**, **17**, 18, **A1** (25),
     G1, **G3** (36)
   insignia **12**, **15**, 19–20, **A1** (25), **G1–3** (35–36)
   National Police Field Force **17**, 19, **G1** (35)
   paratroopers **A1** (24, 25)
   Rangers **11**, **12**, **13**, **14**, **16**, 19, 28,
     G2–3 (35–36)
   scarves 19–20, **G3** (36)

belts 5, 10, 12, 14–15, 21, **A2** (26), **D3** (31)
body armour 7, 9, 14, 17, **E3** (34), **F3** (35),
   G1 (35)

Civilian Irregular Defense Group **A4** (28), 36

equipment 8, **23**
   ammunition belts 10, 14–15
   ammunition pouches 9, **11**, 14, 22–24, **26**,
     33, **E1** (32), **H1** (37)
   ammunition vests 9, **23**
   ARVN rucksacks **3**, **33**
   Grenade Carriers 15, **E1** (32)
   Korean forces **37**
   Lightweight Tropical Rucksack 9, 17, **24**,
     C3 (30), **34**, **H1** (37)
   M1945 Combat Pack 10, **A1** (25), **F1** (34)
   M1956 pattern **6**, **7**, 9, 17, **A4** (28),
     C1 (29–30)
   Marine pack system 15, 17, **E2** (33–34)
   NVA accoutrements **7**, **20**, 22–24, **D** (31)
   NVA rucksacks 24, **B3** (29), **C2** (30), **D1** (31)
   STABO rig **H2** (38–39)
   suspenders 10, **11**, 17, **E1** (32)
   Viet Cong **B** (28–29)

footwear, boots 4, **6**, 12, 18, **A2** (25), **A4** (28),
   C1 (29), **E1** (32), **F1** (34), **F2** (35), **G3** (36)
   sandals 21, **B** (28–29), **D3** (31)

graffiti 8, **E3** (34)
Grenade Carrier Vests **25**, **34**
grenadiers 9, **C3** (30), **34**

headgear
   baseball caps 4–5, **13**, **16**, **A2** (25)
   berets 9, **11**, **15**, 18, 25, **34**, 35, 36,
     H1 (37), 38
   bush hats **11**
   camouflage covers 8, 14, **17**, **C1** (29),
     E2 (33), **F1** (34), **G4** (36)
   fatigue caps 4, **11**, 25
   helicopter crews **A3** (26, 28), **F2–3** (35)
   Marine utility cap **9**, **10**, 11–12
   NVA bush hats 21, **B3** (29), **D2** (31), **35**
   NVA uniform caps 22
   OG 106 Hot Weather Cap 4–5

steel helmets 8, **11**, **14**, 14, **19**, 22, **A1** (25),
   C1 (29), **E2** (33), **F1** (34), **G1** (35), **G3** (36)
stetsons **F2** (35)
sun helmets 21, 22, **28**, **B2** (29), **31**, **D1** (31)
tank crewmen **C2** (30)
Tropical Hats (boonie hats) 5, 9, 12, **13**,
   18, **26**, **38**, **H3** (39)
helicopter crews 14, **16**, **A3** (26, 28),
   F2–3 (34–35), **36**

insignia
   ARVN patches and badges **12**, 19, 20,
     G (35–36)
   name tapes 5–6, **A2** (25), **F2** (34)
   NVA 22, **32**
   of rank 6–7, **9**, **10**, 12, 22, **A1** (25), **32**
   subdued 6–7, **F2** (34)
   unit **A1–2** (25), **F2** (34), 5, 7, 15, 19, 27
   US Marine Corps 11, 12, **E1** (32)
   VN Marine Corps **G4** (36)

Khmer Rouge forces 21
Korean forces 10, **F1** (34), 37

McNamara, Robert S. 4

Nickerson, Lt.Gen. Herman, Jr. 9
Nung mercenaries **A4** (28)
NVA 18, 19, 21, **31**, **D** (31)
   equipment 7, **20**, 22–24, **B3** (29), **30**,
     C2 (30), **D** (31)
   insignia 22, **32**

Pathet Lao forces 21
Pathfinder Detachments 14, **27**

radios 5, 27, **E1** (32), 38

Tet Offensive, 1968: **12**, 22
'Tunnel Rats' 7

uniforms
   ARVN fatigues/utilities 12, 17, 18, 18–19
   camouflage 7–8, **27**, **F1** (34), 37, **H1** (37),
     38, **H3** (39)
     ARVN **12**, **14**, **15**, **16**, **17**, 18, **A1** (25),
       G (35–36)
     'tiger-stripe' **3**, 7, 8, **10**, 12, **A4** (28), **34**,
       35, **G4** (36), **H2** (38)
     US Marine Corps **9**, 12, **E3** (34)
   flight suits 14, **16**, **A3** (26, 28), **F2** (34), **36**
   jackets 4, **6**, 12, **33**
   Jungle Utility Uniform 4, **5**, 12, 18, **C1** (29),
     C3 (30–31)
   Korean forces **F1** (34), 37
   Marine utilities 10–11, 12, **E1** (32)
   NVA 18, 21, **D** (31)
   OG 107 fatigues 4, **5**, **6**, 10, **11**, **12**, 12, **13**,
     A2 (25–6), **33**, **F3** (35)
   T-shirts 5, **7**, 11, 12, **14**

US Navy Rain Jackets 15, **E2** (33)
Viet Cong Main Force 28, **B2–3** (29)
US Army 4–5
   1st Aviation Brigade **F2** (34–35)
   1st Cavalry Division (Airborne) 8, **F3** (35)
   1st Infantry Division 26, **C3** (30–31)
   9th Cavalry **34**
   11th Armored Cavalry **C2** (30)
   101st Airborne Division **3**, **6**, **15**, **C1** (29–30)
   173rd Airborne Brigade 5
   196th Light Infantry Brigade **23**
   advisors **A2** (25–6)
   camouflage uniforms **3**, 7–8, **27**, **34**, **H1** (37)
   equipment **3**, **6**, **7**, **8**, 9–10, 10, **23**, **24**, **26**,
     C1 (29–30), **C3** (30), **34**, **H1** (37),
     H2 (38–39)
   headgear 4–5, **15**, **16**, **A2** (25), **26**,
     C (29–31), **34**, **F2** (35), **H1** (37)
   helicopter crews 14, **16**, **F2–3** (34–35)
   insignia **5**, 5–7, **10**, **A2** (25–6), **27**, **F2** (34)
   Long Range Reconnaissance Patrols (LRRPS)
     8, **15**, **H1** (36–37)
   Special Forces **H2** (38–39)
   tank crewmen **C2** (30)
US Marine Corps 4, **9**, **10**, 10–12, **E** (31–34)
   Combined Action Platoons 12
   equipment 10, 14–15, 17, **E** (32–34)
   headgear **9**, **10**, 11–12, 12, **E2** (33)
   helicopter crews **A3** (26, 28), **36**
   insignia 11, 12, **E1** (32)
   Marine Force Recon units 12
US Navy SEALs **38**, **H3** (39)

Viet Cong **21**, **22**, **28**, **B** (28–29), **29**, 30, **35**
VN Marine Corps 10, **G4** (36)

weapons
   AK–47 **35**
   bayonets 9, 14, **E1** (32)
   Browning Automatic Rifles **A1** (25)
   ChiCom Type 53 carbines 7, **B2** (29)
   ChiCom Type 56 Light Machine Guns **C3** (30)
   ChiCom Type 56 rifles **B3** (29), **D1** (31)
   grenades 9, 9, 15, 24, **A1** (25), **B2** (29),
     C3 (30), **G4** (36), **H1** (37), **H2** (39)
   knives **3**, **23**, **E2** (33), **36**, **H1** (37)
   LAW disposable rocket launchers **6**, **G4** (36)
   M-1 carbines **11**
   M-1 Garand rifles **F1** (34)
   M-2 carbines **A4** (28)
   M-14 rifles **7**, 14, **E1** (32)
   M-16 rifles 7, 8, **C1** (30), **33**, **E3** (34),
     G3 (36), **H2** (39)
   M-60 machine guns 9–10, **38**
   M-79 Grenade Launchers **C3** (30)
   RPG launchers **D2** (31), **35**
   shotguns **38**, **H3** (39)
   XM-177(CAR-15) SMGs **H1** (37)

Yarborough, Lt.Gen. William P. 4